BEFORE TOMORROW

ISBN 979-8-9955183-0-3 (Paperback)

ISBN 979-8-9955183-1-0 (Hardback)

ISBN 979-8-9955183-2-7 (Ebook)

BEFORE

TOMORROW

a memoir by Deb Hazlett

For Joe, Jill, Layeli, and Laci
My family, with all my love.

INTRODUCTION

There was no single moment when I decided to unshackle myself from nearly ninety percent of my belongings, replace them with a travel trailer and a road map, and drive away. It wasn't a sensible plan in any traditional sense. It was simply what I did. Looking back now—across the upheaval, the highs and lows, the adventures and missteps—I'm still a little surprised I did it.

This wasn't a dramatic reinvention or a pilgrimage in search of answers. At sixty-five, the past already had a shape: accepted, sorted, and placed on the *this-is-my-life* shelf. Whatever challenges remained weren't dramatized or avoided; they were managed, day by day.

Selling my house, most of my furniture, and nearly all my belongings—even the clothes I rarely wore—felt like opening a door I had long believed was forbidden, and finally exhaling. In the space that followed, a quieter, unexpected freedom emerged, one I hadn't known was waiting for me. Whatever risk remained felt small beside the peace and maturity that took its place.

For some people, this might not seem like much of a leap. For a woman of my generation, it felt radical.

Being born in the 1950s came with a script already written: marry, be a good wife, raise children, keep a spotless home, be quiet. There was cooking and cleaning and sewing and homework—an endless chain of *ands*. In school, girls took classes designed to prepare us for those expectations. At home, my father taught that a woman's worth came from her husband, that she wasn't "okay" without one.

In seventh grade, I chose drafting, a technical drawing class, as an elective. On the second day of class, two school officials came to the classroom, ushered me out, and walked me to typing. They explained, as if it was simply understood, that drafting was for boys. I had been so absorbed in learning a new way to write numbers that I hadn't noticed I was the only girl. Times have changed, but early messages like that do not fade easily.

Our family had six members: three girls and, finally, a boy—my father's long-awaited son. As the last of the girls, my birth was another disappointment. He never wanted daughters, and he reminded us of that endlessly, sometimes cruelly. He attended my brother's sporting events but never ours. His expectations of his daughters were set at inevitable failure. When failure didn't come, he offered silence instead. My mother once tried to explain, "He doesn't know what to do with girls." Looking back now, I suspect he was simply repeating the narrow world he had been raised in, a place where sons mattered and daughters quietly stayed in the background.

Growing up, the idea that I would never be enough—or could never succeed—simply because I wasn't a boy lodged itself inside me like a lie I didn't yet have the language to question. I didn't understand it as inequality then; I felt it as an unease, a sense of being slightly out of place, as if something in my alignment had been off from the beginning.

I saw versions of it everywhere. I remember a brilliant friend in high school who earned high marks and a scholarship. Her father refused to let her accept it, saying it would be wasted on a woman. At the time, no one questioned it.

Over the years, as I grew into myself, I slowly learned to turn down that sense of never being enough, like lowering the volume on a radio.

But in my youth, running away became my way of coping with the internal disturbance. My first attempt came when I was five years old. I only made it to the corner. In first grade, feeling broken, I walked away from school for three hours before being found. It continued through middle school. At fifteen, the discomfort was so overwhelming that I managed to stay gone for a month. Running and hiding wove themselves into the fabric of who I was. Some might trace my late-in-life desire to step outside acceptable boundaries back to those early years, but blame has its own box on the shelf.

My childhood was far from ideal by today's standards, but it was not unusual for my generation. Life eventually taught me that the past is unchangeable and best left where it belongs. Healing, I came to understand, happens most reliably in the everyday. Life is too precious not to seek harmony between who you are and how you live.

By sixty-five, my truth had crystallized: conventional life was suffocating me. I had a suburban house by the park, two children, two granddaughters, and a decent retirement from a public agency. On paper, everything fit. In reality, my life felt like a round peg forced into a square hole. A low, persistent thrum of urgency had become impossible to ignore. Adventure and challenge felt less like indulgence and more like necessity—not for escape, but for alignment.

This wasn't a midlife crisis. It was a shift into a life that finally made room for my restlessness. I was breaking nearly every generational rule I had been programmed to follow—and I knew it.

At sixty-five, towing and living alone in a trailer—exploring the country without a definitive plan—became my map to freedom. Alongside that decision grew a deeper faith, not loud or performative, but steady. My goal was simple: remove every restraint possible and step fully into the life I had been dreaming of.

Friends and family were bewildered. Many were certain I didn't know what I was doing—that failure was inevitable, that it was unsafe for a woman my age to travel alone. Their concerns weren't without basis, but they also revealed how little faith they had in me. What few understood was how far my research, preparation, and mental resolve had already carried me. Learning to tow and understand the mechanics of a trailer was simply another skill to acquire. Others had done it. So could I. My common sense hadn't abandoned me. The power behind my *why* outweighed their doubts.

Choosing this direction felt natural. Travel had always called to me, feeding my curiosity and sense of possibility.

The realization arrived during a trip to the Highlands of Scotland. My granddaughter and I were walking along a lakeshore across from the Black Isle near Dingwall. The air carried a refreshing coolness; warm sweaters were necessary. The scent of water and grass rose around us, clean and unmistakable. Before us lay rolling fields of wheat, soft green hills, and mountains resting quietly in the distance.

This was not the dramatic Highlands I had imagined. It was gentler, calmer, and deeply moving. Standing there, I understood something I hadn't considered before: my own country held places just as beautiful and just as worthy of wonder. A shift was taking place. The restlessness I had learned to manage no longer felt like a flaw—it was an invitation with direction. The thought appeared quietly but refused to leave: I could go see them myself. Perhaps it wasn't too late after all.

The lower forty-eight states stretched out with endless landscapes and possibilities. Research only deepened my eagerness to drive coastlines, roam the Rockies, wander the Blue Ridge Parkway, breathe in the Smoky Mountains, follow music, and perhaps find a path where that restless ache might finally soften. If nothing else, I knew the road would offer extraordinary moments.

The traveling life became my antidote—and remains so. It didn't frighten me. It awakened me.

CHAPTER 1 — THE THRESHOLD

The choice was not offered—but the understanding was

What should have been a simple, same-day medical procedure became an extraordinary event—one that quietly but decisively altered my understanding of what it means to live honestly within a human life. It was as though a harsh, unrelenting light had suddenly exposed the distance between how cautiously I had been living at the edges of my life and how far I was from living in alignment with my spiritual self.

About a year into my cancer treatment, a medical issue arose that required a pacemaker. I was told it was a straightforward procedure, one that would have me in and out in no time at all. I had seen it firsthand; my father had undergone the same surgery and returned home within a few hours.

While recovering and waiting to be released, I was informed that I would instead be transferred to intensive care overnight for observation. No explanation was offered—only that these were the doctor's orders. Because the regular ICU was full due to COVID, I was moved to an improvised unit that felt nearly abandoned, staffed by only two nurses. The open area held a faint antiseptic smell, the kind that lingers in places reopened after too long, and the overhead lights hummed dimly in the quiet. The few beds were separated by curtains. I soon learned that even the hospital laboratory didn't know where the unit was located.

Two or three hours into the night, I woke to the steady rhythm of a monitor nearby and asked to use the restroom. A nurse adjusted my lines, and I walked there on my own. On the way back, he remarked on how well I was moving. I laughed and told him there was nothing wrong with my legs. I asked for a Tylenol, mentioning that the area felt a little sore.

When he opened my gown to examine the incision, he stopped. A hematoma—already the size of a grapefruit—had formed and was pushing upward toward my neck. The energy in the room shifted instantly. The quiet space filled with hurried voices and the sharp rustle of medical gloves. What had been routine and calm erupted into urgency. Both nurses tried repeatedly to reach a cardiologist, then any physician at all. No one responded.

Without authorization to administer pain medication beyond Tylenol, one nurse handed me a cloth and told me to bite down. He warned me it was going to hurt. I remember begging that I could not die—not then. My daughter had just lost her father only days before. She hadn't even buried him yet. The thought of her losing another parent so soon was unbearable.

One nurse braced me while the other pressed into the hematoma again and again, using steady, forceful pressure in an attempt to stop the bleeding. Each push sent a fresh wave of pain through me, immediate and consuming. I remained fully conscious as it continued—push after push—for nearly half an hour. I whimpered, unable to do anything else, waiting for it to end.

What followed remains fragmented in my memory. Additional medical staff arrived. Medication was administered—vague recollections of lights and intercom announcements. I felt myself receding inward, becoming smaller. Then there was nothing.

During that stretch of unconsciousness, I had an experience that I'm not sure belonged entirely to this world. I found myself standing with my back to the edge of a cliff, my bare heels pressed into the rock. There was no sound, no scent, no taste—only a profound stillness.

Ahead of me lay gentle green hills dotted with trees, like those you might find in an orchard. I felt the heaviness of human life, as if a thousand-pound weight had joined gravity to anchor me more firmly to the earth.

Behind me stretched a canyon so vast its depth dissolved into darkness. It held a serenity and stillness unlike anything I had ever known. I felt an overwhelming pull to enter that peace, to belong to it. I understood, without reasoning or fear, that if I leaned back even slightly, I would fall into its quiet embrace.

The choice, however, was not offered.

About a year later, while walking with a friend, I shared this experience. She sent me a passage describing our eternal and human lives as two expressions of the same soul—two sides of a single coin. The words settled quietly within me. Perhaps the cliff had revealed both at once: the gravity of being human and the light of spirit.

The effect of my vision did not change me abruptly, but it changed me decisively. From that point forward, my thoughts began circling a central question: how to weave that same sense of levity and tranquility into this life.

CHAPTER 2 — PREPARING THE BODY

The body deserves the same respect as the dream

My health came first. After everything my body had already carried me through, I owed it that respect. Being of sound mind and body was not something I took lightly. It was the first true checkmark on my list.

Stepping on the scale stung more than I wanted to admit. Age has a way of arriving politely, as if asking permission. Then, one morning, you realize it has unpacked its bags and moved in. Post-menopause had left its calling card. If I were going to take my life on the road, I needed an honest inventory of the body I was bringing with me.

So I did the sensible thing: I went to the doctor. Before trusting myself to haul a trailer across state lines, wrestle a heavy hitch into place, or climb in and out of a truck bed with generators or a fire pit balanced awkwardly in my arms, I wanted a professional opinion. Not that I expected her to be thrilled, but I hoped she wouldn't try to sedate me for my own safety.

We talked through what I was planning—the physical exertion, the solitude, the open-ended timeline. When she asked how long I imagined traveling, the only answer that felt honest was "until I don't want to anymore." She assessed my mental health with a calm seriousness that suggested she was prepared for any answer. The evaluation was more involved than I had anticipated, but I suppose that's what happens when you announce, at sixty-five, you are uprooting your life on purpose.

She wanted to be sure I was of sound mind, not just sound body.

I passed, which was encouraging.

There was blood work, an eye exam, an X-ray, and one referral. I left with a stack of pamphlets about healthy eating, as if vegetables were a revelation. What I really needed was a practical way to eat on the road, where a kitchen is more of a concept than a location.

Could I have prepared more? Learned every detail of the kitchen area, perfected my diet, mapped out a thorough plan? Of course. Did I? Absolutely not.

Instead, I leaned on my long history of road trips: an ice chest, bread, peanut butter, lunch meat, snacks, and an unapologetic amount of water. And coffee—the heartbeat of my mornings. I couldn't decide which coffee maker to bring, so I brought three. Some decisions don't require sacrifice.

Cooking without a stable kitchen felt intimidating at first—no full refrigerator, little counter space, and a stove that required negotiation rather than simple operation. But travel teaches quickly. I packed the basics—spices, bread, sugar, flour, and oil—enough to keep myself fed even when the nearest town was more theoretical than actual.

Movement mattered, perhaps more than anything else. Swimming had always been a refuge. Back home, there was a heated saltwater Olympic-sized pool, and early mornings were reserved for adults. Then the water was calm and warm, like stepping into silk. I would miss it more than I expected. I have yet to find another pool quite like it, but there were enough places along the road to keep my body from settling permanently into the shape of the driver's seat.

I've never been a runner, but walking has always suited me. So I increased it. Two miles became three, then four. A few days a week became nearly every day. When the weather made the outdoors unappealing, I turned to a walking video called *Walk at Home*. It wasn't glamorous, but it kept me moving, and moving was a promise I had to keep to myself.

By the time my physical was signed off, something had settled into place. I wasn't training for endurance or reinvention. I was simply ensuring that the body I lived in could support the life I was about to ask of it. Walking became routine. Strength followed slowly. Confidence arrived last. I didn't yet know how often I would rely on all three once the road finally began.

Even with all that preparation, strength alone wasn't enough. With my body cleared and capable, the question remained whether the rest of my life could be simplified with the same care.

Before I could leave, I needed a clear understanding of the finances as well.

CHAPTER 3 — PREPARING THE FINANCES

Freedom asks for faith and arithmetic

My walks around the park and neighborhood became about more than strengthening my legs. I turned the music down in my headphones, and my thoughts drifted toward the possibilities and decisions ahead. With each step, day after day, practical questions rose and settled, and what had felt scattered began, little by little, to take shape.

Being clear-headed and physically capable was reassuring. It was a steady stone in the foundation of what I was building. That was the first step. The second was my finances. For better or worse, they would determine what kind of future was even possible.

There were two piles to consider: what I would have once everything was sold, and what this new life would require of me. In theory, my goal was simple—clear titles and no debt. In practice, the path toward that simplicity was anything but straightforward.

The truth was uncomplicated, if not easy: wanderlust and financial reality often live in separate worlds. One wants freedom; the other wants receipts. For this to work, they would have to learn how to coexist.

My first task was to understand what I truly owned—not just the objects occupying rooms, but the assets capable of carrying the weight of a new beginning. I planned to use my home's equity to clear remaining debt and secure clear titles for both the trailer and the tow vehicle. With a seller's net sheet and a trade-in estimate for my SUV laid out in front of me, the ground beneath my feet felt a little more solid—less imagined, more real.

There were other pillars—savings and retirement accounts—but I set them aside. They were my unspoken reserves, the safety net that whispered I wasn't entirely reckless. Even after the blogs, articles, and books I devoured—and the hours spent learning systems and practices—I remained aware of how much I didn't know. That unknowing made a backup essential.

I gathered every figure I could and laid them out plainly. I needed to see the whole picture, to know whether I was standing on solid ground or stepping into quicksand that might give way beneath me. When the final numbers settled into place, the relief was steady and physical—like slipping into warm saltwater for a long swim, the kind that loosens muscles and allows the body to exhale. Seeing the truth in its uncomplicated form grounded me.

But numbers were only the beginning. The harder work came next: deciding what to let go.

People like to say simplifying saves money. Sometimes that's true. But trailers come with their own list of demands.

There was more to account for than the purchase price: maintenance, insurance, fuel for the truck that would pull it, and repairs that would inevitably arrive at the worst possible moment. Even freedom requires responsibility.

With the larger decisions made, I built a budget. Budget might be too dignified a word; it was more of a hopeful sketch. Gas, food, campsites, insurance, emergencies, and a column labeled simply: *Life Happens*. It felt like drawing a map while knowing the landscape ahead was still fogbound. Beneath the numbers lingered quieter questions: What if I miscalculated? What if something broke in the middle of nowhere? What if I ran out of money?

As with preparing my body, honesty was the only path forward. If I wanted this life—the road, the quiet, the open horizon—then my finances had to be prepared with the same clarity. I upgraded my AAA membership to its highest tier, including coverage for the trailer. A small gesture, perhaps, but one that offered real reassurance.

Leaving my house also meant leaving an address behind, and mail is designed for people who stay rooted. Before I left, I rented a private mailbox so I could remain reachable without staying anchored—forwarding what mattered and letting the rest fall away. When I knew I would pass through a town, mail could meet me there through general delivery, one of those quiet systems designed for people in motion. Everything else moved online. It wasn't complicated, but it was essential. It turned out that even paperwork has weight, and setting some of it down felt like freedom.

Once everything had been listed, estimated, questioned, and reviewed again, another shift occurred. The numbers themselves hadn't changed. But I had.

The foundation beneath me felt firm—not born of fantasy, but of intention. I realized I wasn't preparing out of fear or planning for scarcity. This wasn't about limitations. It was about possibilities. And possibility is worth the effort.

What came next was twofold. First, I needed to choose the vessel that would carry this new version of my life—whether that meant a van, a motorhome, or a trailer hitched to a future I could tow behind me. The second had little to do with numbers at all. It would require releasing—paring down the world I had lived in so the life ahead would have room to breathe.

Letting go wasn't just a financial decision; it was emotional triage. Each item seemed to ask its own quiet questions: Do I still want your memory? Will I need you where I'm going? More often than not, the answer drifted toward no.

By the time my home went on the market, most of the life I had built there had already been released. The next decision would determine everything: what kind of home I would carry with me—and how well it would carry me.

CHAPTER 4 — A LIFE I COULD TOW

Every new life begins with imagining the shape

Once my finances were on solid ground, the next step wasn't letting go of my belongings—not yet. First, I had to choose the physical shape of my new world: the trailer and the tow vehicle.

Before I ever set foot on an RV lot, I spent months online falling down the joyful, chaotic rabbit hole of recreational vehicles. I learned the difference between 30-amp and 50-amp service easily enough. But the solar systems—the inverters, the converters, the language of voltage and power—felt like something that should come with a decoder ring. I skimmed articles, dove into forums, read blog posts written by people with usernames like RoadGoddess74 and BoondockBrody62, and watched far too many videos about tank sizes, propane capacity, and hitching options for dummies.

What I didn't realize at the time was that understanding something in theory and knowing where the switch is were very different things.

It was overwhelming and entertaining in equal measure. But beneath it all, something sparked—a quiet sense that I was beginning to learn the language of a life I hadn't yet lived.

Eventually, I took my research into the real world.

My favorite excursion was the massive RV show in Portland, Oregon. I was so excited, you'd think I was headed to Disneyland. Well—maybe not Disneyland. But an unforgettable concert at Red Rocks? Absolutely. The place felt like a music festival where every artist was an RV. Aisles of gleaming rigs stretched endlessly, each one distinctive in its own way.

I toured Class A motorhomes even though they were never a serious contender. Sitting behind the wheel, the sheer mass of the thing—and the idea that I would be responsible for guiding it down a highway—felt a little overwhelming. But walking through them was another experience entirely. I ran my fingers over gleaming countertops and polished cabinetry, amazed at what people were calling *camping*. Full-sized refrigerators. Fireplaces. Washers and dryers. Bedrooms with real doors that closed.

I practically drooled my way through them.

But I knew myself. I wasn't looking for an apartment on wheels—not alone. Maybe someday. Not now.

Class A motorhomes and large fifth wheels dropped off my list quickly. Too big. Too heavy. Too complicated. And I had no interest in acquiring a special license just to drive my house around.

Class B vans—the conversions—were seriously tempting. I even traveled to Las Vegas to tour a warehouse where they were being built. I climbed inside one and stood in the middle, turning slowly to take it all in. A dedicated queen bed, which was on my list. A bathroom—technically. What they called a *wet bath*, meaning the shower head hung over the toilet and every inch of space had multiple purposes. Clever. Compact. Efficient. Everything within arm's reach.

They stayed on my list for quite a while.

Until I imagined myself trapped inside one during a long storm. Cooking dinner in a space the size of a generous broom closet while rain hammered the roof. Dishes stacked in a sink barely large enough for a salad bowl. Wanting to stretch out with nowhere to go.

The image lingered.

For the freedom I was craving, it felt too tight. Too confining.

Next came Class C motorhomes. They offered more breathing room than the vans: a larger bathroom, workable living space, and the sense that daily life might unfold more comfortably inside one. I considered them seriously for their simplicity and independence, without yet realizing how much the details would matter. Things like built-in generators—something I would only understand much later, after experience had done what research failed to do.

Sometimes what you haven't yet learned would have been very useful information yesterday.

But Class C motorhomes came with one complication I couldn't ignore: towing a car. Two engines to worry about instead of one. That was enough to stop me. I was not even remotely mechanically inclined. I didn't need the odds doubled.

So I turned my attention to what felt simplest: the travel trailer.

One engine.

One vehicle.

One set of responsibilities.

A home I could tow, detach, and leave behind while I explored.

The more I imagined myself living in each option, the clearer it became that the trailer made the most sense. Independent. Manageable. Practical. That was the moment I shifted from dreaming to being smart about this.

I began researching construction: quality, longevity, insulation, and the dreaded topic of leaking windows. I lost count of how many online posts I read about window leaks and failing slide-outs, those expandable sections that make a trailer feel almost roomy. Every time I imagined a slide malfunctioning while I was alone in a campground, the mental picture was always the same: me standing helplessly—probably in the rain—while the slide dangled at a forty-degree angle and raccoons looked on with judgment.

I made a decision. No slide-outs. None.

My first true non-negotiable.

As I walked through trailer after trailer, I developed a habit. I pushed on the walls—literally. If a wall flexed too much or gave off a wobble that suggested it was held together by hope and staples, I walked out.

If looking, touching, and feeling could tell me something important, I intended to listen.

Somewhere during a late-night online deep dive, I stumbled into the world of Airstreams—and everything changed.

I landed on their website and watched a how-it's-built video. I was riveted. The aluminum shell. The curves. The craftsmanship. It was unlike anything I had seen.

I dove into Airstream forums and noticed something else: the familiar complaints—leaks, failing slide-outs, flexing walls—didn't appear with the same frequency. People still complained—it's the internet—but the issues were different, less structural.

Airstreams were solid. Durable. Beautiful.

And they had no slide-outs.

My non-negotiable.

That's when I knew. I had fallen for Airstreams.

I began studying floor plans and visiting the local dealership. At first, I considered the sixteen-foot: adorable, simple, nostalgic. Then the nineteen-foot. Eventually I reached the twenty-two-foot and decided that was it.

I brought my son to see it.

He walked through, nodded, stepped out, and stepped into the next model.

"Mom," he said, "look at the twenty-three-foot."

That one had two axles—a detail I hadn't yet understood the importance of.

He had.

But then, he drives a fire engine up and down the streets of San Francisco.

A few days later my friend Bev joined me. She nodded thoughtfully as she considered my choice, then stepped around into the twenty-five-foot and declared,

"Deb, this one is yours."

She was right.

The difference between the trailers wasn't just the layout or a handful of extra steps. In daily life, it was monumental. The twenty-five-foot offered wraparound windows, the table at one end and the bedroom at the other—room to breathe—and two axles. Stability. Safety. Ease of towing.

By then, I was balancing practicality against the unforgiving reality of the price tag. Airstreams were undeniably more expensive—sometimes triple the cost.

That's what led me to Airstream Marketplace.

There I found a gently used twenty-five-foot International owned by a couple who had purchased it during COVID. They'd taken it out a few times, realized trailer life wasn't for them, and decided to sell. It already had solar panels, a high-end inverter system, and upgrades I would have added myself. Financially, it made far more sense.

I purchased her in Southern California while I was still up north. The clear title arrived overnight. I insured her. Arranged delivery.

And when she arrived, I stepped inside and thought,

This is home.

Compared with choosing the trailer, selecting the tow vehicle felt almost secondary.

I understood that sufficient towing capacity was non-negotiable. I knew my fully loaded trailer would weigh around seven thousand pounds. I learned about tongue weight, payload, hitches, and ratios—concepts I had barely glanced at months earlier.

Then one day I drove to a dealership to look at Dodge Rams.

Sitting out front was a green 1500 Hemi eTorque.

My favorite color. Nature's color. The color of life.

No one approached me. No swarm of salespeople. My hand was practically raised, silently begging, *please sell me this truck.*

Not a soul was around.

It turned out the dealership had just been sold and was closed for the transition. I had somehow wandered onto a car lot the single day there were no salespeople working.

I stood with that green truck for a long time. I checked the weights on my phone. Reviewed towing capacity. Ran numbers. Everything aligned with the trailer. I circled it like a bird inspecting its nest.

That was it.

That was the moment.

I returned the next morning and was waiting when they opened.

I chose the tow vehicle the same way I once chose the Green Bay Packers in an office football pool—because I liked the color.

(I won that pool, by the way.)

Sometimes the math defines what's possible, and instinct chooses within it.

CHAPTER 5 — THE QUIET UNRAVELING

Letting go is its own kind of becoming

Downsizing wasn't a single event; it was a slow unraveling—quiet in some corners, loud and messy in others. While I was learning about axles and amps and tongue weight in one world, I was sorting through generations of memory in the other. The choices and plans began to synchronize, as if fate—or something kinder—were quietly clearing the path. Even the contractor I'd hired to prepare the house for market showed up a week early.

In hindsight, the pattern was clear. I was living two realities at once: the one I was choosing and the one I was carefully dismantling.

Once the trailer and the truck were decided, my house became an ecosystem of shifting piles. A room would look normal one day and hollow the next. I'd open a drawer and feel as though I'd begun an archaeological dig, each object holding a story that required a decision: keep, carry, or release.

After my parents passed, their belongings lived in boxes in my garage—years of their lives waiting quietly for me to decide their fate. Sorting through them had been slow, tender work. I passed along what belonged to siblings or grandchildren. The rest I stored—not because I needed the items, but because discarding them felt too sharp, too final. Grief, I realized, has its own economy.

Now I was faced with the same reckoning, only this time it was my life spread out before me. I wondered whether my children, confronted with these choices someday, would make the same ones I was making now. It is astonishing how many belongings remain simply because they once held meaning: furniture inherited or tied to earlier versions of myself, clothing that no longer fits my present body, shelves of just-in-case items.

I reserved a ten-by-ten storage unit, roughly the size of a small bedroom, which I imagined would neatly contain the parts of my life that still mattered. It felt comforting, like leaving a nightlight on for a version of myself who might visit someday.

It filled rather quickly.

The bartering came unexpectedly but soon became one of my favorite parts of the process. I traded the washer and dryer for moving help, my entertainment center for carpet cleaning, garden equipment for hauling, a patio shelf for an extra set of hands. It was as if the world itself were rearranging, object by object, preparing me for what came next.

The house went on the market sooner than expected. It was one of those dizzying markets where homes sold in days, sometimes hours, and mine was no exception. One moment I was watching the contractor patch nail holes and touch up trim; the next, I had an accepted offer before I'd fully processed what was happening.

Suddenly, everything had a deadline, and the pieces were falling into place. It almost felt settled.

Three days before I had to be out of the house, the day after most everything had been moved into storage, I tested positive for COVID.

Not the mild version—the flattened, fevered, breathless kind where walking to the bathroom felt like an accomplishment. It was the borderline version where, at my age, I could easily end up in the hospital if I didn't stop. I had been running on adrenaline and checklists, and my body finally refused to keep pace.

My daughter, Jillian, was FaceTiming from Southern California when she noticed my cough again—how I looked—and questioned my temperature. She insisted I take a test. I resisted; I didn't have time to be sick. She had the test kit delivered to me, and I relented.

When the second line appeared, dread washed over me, followed by a strange surrender.

Jill was already calling her brother, and decisions were made within minutes.

I didn't have the option to fall apart.

So I simply… wilted.

My son Joe arrived within hours, mask on, worried eyes, steady voice. My friend Bev—dear, practical Bev—showed up the next morning, armed with food, cleaning supplies, and the kind of quiet authority that helped me believe everything would be okay.

I spent those days on an air mattress in my empty bedroom, sweating through fever after fever, a fog settling through my brain, the room echoing with every cough. With the furniture already gone, the house sounded hollow, every movement and breath bouncing off the walls. Joe and Bev moved through the house like gentle phantoms. When they weren't packing, loading the truck, or cleaning, they slid food and fluids across the floor and checked on me from a careful distance.

In the evenings, Joe would sit on the hallway floor outside my door, leaning against the wall, and we would talk.

Sometimes it was about practical things—whether the storage unit was full, whether the truck was ready—but other times he would remind me of things from our past.

Once he laughed and said, "Mom, do you remember when we played *let's get lost* in San Francisco?"

I did remember, and it had been an exceptionally fun day. Apparently, adventure had been my parenting style long before I owned a trailer.

Those conversations were soft, tender, and unexpectedly peaceful— small pockets of connection inside the storm. Rare moments when being taken care of didn't feel like failure. It felt like family.

When the day came to hand over the house keys and pick up the trailer, I was still feverish and deep in the illness. I took as much Tylenol as was safe, put on a mask, and drove to the storage lot where my Airstream waited.

The person handing it over tried earnestly to explain how everything worked, but nothing was sinking in. I felt weaker by the minute. I watched the hitching process the way you watch a foreign film without subtitles—aware things were happening, aware they mattered, absorbing almost nothing.

But the trailer was hitched.

The clear title was in my hand.

There was no turning back.

I climbed into the truck, glanced in the rearview mirror, and saw my new home following faithfully.

I had expected to feel triumph—everything, all at once.

Instead, I felt sick—but determined.

Highway 80 blurred past in construction cones and adrenaline. I drove slowly and carefully, like someone carrying something precious on her back—which, in a way, I was. My son followed behind me, with Bev and her husband behind him, a small convoy of love and concern.

Forty-odd miles later, feverish and exhausted, I rolled into Napa and into Skyline Wilderness Park.

My house was gone. My body was weak. And my new home was following quietly behind me.

I couldn't see it then, but those first days living in the trailer were still the beginning. I wasn't going anywhere. I was unwell, moving slowly, measuring my time in sunrises, morning coffee, and hours of sleep.

The road could wait.

But even in that stillness, something had quietly shifted.

CHAPTER 6 — THE FIRST MORNING OF FREEDOM

Every beginning asks for a surrender—even if it arrives wrapped in fever

Skyline Wilderness Park nestles against the rolling hills of southeast Napa, with vineyards stretching northward. My windows faced east, toward the rising light. It was mid-March, and winter still held the land in its cool embrace. Rain had transformed the usually golden slopes into a living green, the hills breathing again. Many of the trees stood bare, their pale branches lifted like quiet offerings, while others held their color—deep, steady, unwilling to let go. A hush moved through the park, soft and deliberate, as if the season itself were pausing between breaths.

On the first morning of freedom from the weight of society's expectations, I woke with a blistering headache, an irritating cough, and a fever still simmering beneath my skin. I didn't care. I shuffled from the bed to the table, drew the curtains wide along the wraparound windows, made a cup of coffee, and sat down.

The view—the hills, the trees, the vineyards—was spectacular. But what settled most deeply into me was not the scenery; it was how extraordinary it felt simply to be there. I felt special. Lucky. Like an outlaw, finally choosing a life I had never been given permission to live. Sick as I was, I had never felt more grateful to be alive.

Even with COVID still moving through my body, pride rose in my chest. Somehow, I felt welcome.

After a few minutes, I stepped out of my new home into the crisp morning air. It cooled my overheated skin. I sat at the picnic table, sipping coffee and breathing in the scent of dew on the grass. Only a handful of trailers were in the park that time of year. I watched squirrels race up and down the trees while the maintenance crew began their day. I tired quickly, but even the symptoms couldn't interrupt the shift unfolding within me.

It felt like the earliest moment of bloom—quiet, tentative, and real.

What I didn't know then was that morning coffee outside my trailer would become a ritual, one of my favorite times of day. It was in those quiet moments that I found my footing for the hours ahead.

I loved watching the dogs on their morning walks through the park, most of them friendly and eager to stop and say hello. Their owners passed with easy nods or brief greetings. I enjoyed watching other campers hitch up and leave for their own destinations—vacationers, retirees on planned routes, their return dates already marked.

I wasn't passing through. I had stepped outside the usual lanes and into a life without an itinerary or an end date. Morning and evening, this rhythm grounded me—the simplicity of beginnings and endings.

The first two weeks were nothing like I had planned, but I adjusted quickly. In my original vision, I would have completed a full orientation at home: parking the trailer in front of my house, practicing every system, moving in slowly and confidently. By the time I reached Napa, I imagined all that would remain were goodbyes and small discoveries. I had mapped that time down to the hour. Then I would hit the road alone, discovery as my compass.

Instead, after savoring that first morning, I dressed, masked up, and went to the grocery store. I felt worse than I had in days. Whether it was the illness itself or the accumulated strain of exhaustion and change, everything narrowed to one simple truth: my body needed rest. With food to last a few days, I crawled back into bed and allowed myself to heal.

The first stretch of my wanderer's life was simply that: rest.

Skyline Park had nearly ten hiking trails and a Native Habitat Garden. The rains had brushed the hills with soft green, though the plants and shrubs still lingered in winter's sleep. Each morning, I made coffee and sat outside with the dew, absorbing the quiet wonder around me. Then I returned to bed.

The land's slow awakening mirrored my own. This life change hadn't arrived with a clear mission or declaration; it felt more like a presence, gently guiding me. I leaned heavily on faith.

By the second week, energy returned in small increments. I unpacked and cleaned in short bursts, here and there, when I had the strength. It became another kind of unraveling, sorting through the last of my belongings. I organized what clearly belonged and set aside what didn't. Once again, I found myself with piles to donate, bags to discard, and a short list of essentials still missing.

Minimizing, for me, isn't nearly as simple as it sounds. But little by little, the trailer became my home.

As a finishing touch, I arranged a small bouquet of fresh flowers in a mason jar and placed it in the front wraparound window. Another shift. The space no longer felt temporary. It held the warmth of home.

I ended up staying in the area for a month, two weeks to heal, and another two for what I had originally planned. Skyline had a two-week stay limit and required campers to leave for seven days before returning. So I moved the trailer for a week—my first experience hitching and unhitching.

My granddaughter, Layeli, flew up to join me, and my son helped with the hitch.

I chose Solano Lake for that week. The RV sites were rougher than Skyline's, and the bathrooms were a little frightening for a beginner. A year later, my perspective would change completely; now, I seek those quieter, less polished parks.

The time with my oldest granddaughter was a gift. We explored, talked, read, ate, and napped. My body needed that gentleness. Our favorite part of the park wasn't the lake; it was the wild, bold, noisy peacocks strutting everywhere. *Shy* is not a word one would ever associate with them.

Before we headed back to Napa for my final preparations, my fourteen-year-old granddaughter asked a question that seemed to come from nowhere.

"Gma, does this mean you're trying to run away from everything?"

I should have been surprised. I wasn't. Layeli had always been observant in ways that could catch me off guard.

When I asked why she thought that, she explained we shared a special bond and she worried my leaving might break it. She was afraid I'd be gone for months, that I wouldn't see her, that I might not remember her, or not miss her. Looking at her beautiful face, I felt the ache settle deep in my chest.

Her question stayed with me longer than she knew. For much of my life, movement had been my answer when things became difficult. But this felt different. I wasn't leaving anything behind. I was stepping toward something I had never allowed myself to want.

I hugged her and assured her I could never forget her; that it would take something happening to my mind for that. I reminded her she had recently moved four hundred miles away and nothing had broken our bond yet. Why would traveling do that?

She didn't understand why I was doing it, and I tried to explain. I talked about how this was something I had been too afraid to want earlier in my life and about the experiences I hoped to have. She listened, working to understand. With little thought—and before asking her mother, as I should have—I invited her to join me for a week or two over the summer.

Before I left Napa, I was blessed to share a meal with my children and grandchildren. My daughter, Jill, drove over four hundred miles from Southern California to see me off. That alone told me how much the moment meant. It was Easter weekend, my last weekend there. I sat at the table, looking over the family I had created: my son, my daughter, their partners, and my two beautiful granddaughters. We had weathered storms together and come through changed for the better—stronger.

I reflected on a recent season when it felt as though we were being pulled apart in every direction. Two of the strongest forces were my father nearing the end of his life and my own battle with breast cancer. Two nights before my surgery, my son, my daughter, and I sat together, nerves frayed nearly to the breaking point. I gathered them close and said what felt true: we were being hit from all sides, and the only way through was to hold tightly to one another, keep putting one foot in front of the other, have faith, and know that we would endure.

And we did. A double mastectomy. Pneumonia two days later. My father's passing the following day. And there was more. It was a brutal season, but we survived it together.

Now, as I prepared to step into this new way of living, we were together again, still holding on.

Both my children worried about me and the direction I was taking. But perhaps because of what we had already endured, and what we had learned we could survive, they didn't try to stop me. They stood with me.

With my father's passing, the remaining threads of generational limitations—and their quiet authority—simply dissolved. I removed the societal blinders, respectfully placing their remains in a box on the shelf. I finally felt free to grant myself permission to do and be anything I chose. I no longer needed to hide.

While that permission may take time to settle fully within me, it was what guided me here, to this campground, on this day. And it was here that I would begin to discover what I was truly made of.

CHAPTER 7 — THEORY VS. REALITY

The application of knowledge typically requires common sense

It was a partly cloudy morning—neither too cool nor too warm, with no hint the weather might turn either way. A light breeze touched the bare branches, and the rolling green hills shimmered with early dew. Squirrels were already up, racing through the park. Good traveling weather.

I had said the last of my goodbyes the day before; this morning was mine alone. I sat outside at the table with my coffee, absorbing the quiet atmosphere of the park. The reality of leaving my home area behind filled me with a nervous anticipation. I was really doing this.

I sorted the inside of the trailer and hitched on my own. After a visit to the dump station to clean my tanks, I climbed behind the wheel and eased out of Skyline Park. Before turning onto the road, I paused and glanced back at where I had been.

A subtle flush moved through me, almost indistinct—more wonder than emotion.

One of those rare moments when everything feels perfect and you wish time would stand still—the kind of quiet lift rising from somewhere deep inside. It holds you there for just a breath before the world begins moving again.

Holding onto the feeling, quietly praying my gratitude, I shifted into drive and left the familiar behind.

Over the previous weeks, *Traveler* had become my theme song. I turned it up and put it on repeat as I made my cautious way out of

Napa, through Jameson Canyon, onto Highway 80 with its endless construction maze, then to I-505, and finally I-5 north. Sitting high in the cab of the truck, the trailer steady behind me, I felt as if I had risen to some marvelous plane where the noise of ordinary life simply fell away. I sang along, smiling at the absurd joy of it.

The lyrics echoed the wanderlust I was learning to welcome. This wasn't about chasing anything. I just needed to go. The first leg of my travels was Vancouver Island to visit my sister Sandy, but how I got there hardly mattered—it was the traveling itself I craved. Somewhere along the way I had discovered a quiet place inside myself, and it felt as if something there had finally been set free, hollering a carefree yippee into the open road.

Armed with too much research and no practical application, I boldly—or perhaps ignorantly—chose to dry camp at my first destination away from home. Black Butte Lake was a U.S. Army Corps of Engineers campground with no electrical or water hookups. I'd been told my trailer had a sophisticated solar system capable of handling it. That was the full extent of my understanding.

I learned quickly that all my theoretical reading was useless without the practical knowledge of locating a single switch for that sophisticated system. The battery wouldn't hold a charge and drained almost immediately. I hadn't read much about batteries and was beginning to suspect I should have focused less on what the system *could* do and more on how to actually use it. I pushed buttons I thought had something to do with solar, staring at the small glowing control panel, waiting for something—anything—to happen. Nothing did.

Thankfully, I had extra blankets and heavy socks, but the realization landed like lightning: some things I thought I understood, I clearly did not.

The next day bore no resemblance to the explorations I'd imagined. Instead, it filled with manuals, phone calls, and internet searches, a familiar déjà vu of plans unraveling. I tried plugging the trailer into the truck and letting it run. I tried everything I could think of. Nothing worked.

It took about twenty-four hours for it to sink in, reluctantly, that the battery itself was bad. So much for the inspection I'd purchased before picking up the trailer. I wondered what else that inadequate service might have missed. One thing I knew for certain, I would find out.

Eventually, I gave up and walked by the lake. My thoughts circled where I was, what I was doing, and the battery and power issues that had already announced themselves on the first day. It would have been easier not to be alone, to have someone to talk it through with, someone to share the weight of it. I knew that.

But the truth was, I was alone—and I had been for a while. Wanting to lean on someone, especially in the way women of my generation had been taught, didn't help me here. What still surprised me was how quickly that instinct surfaced, how natural the pull remained, even after all the time and independence I had earned.

A memory from long ago surfaced, catching me off guard. It was a day at Disneyland, near closing time. The parade was passing, and I stood off to the side watching my children's faces light up. Their excitement was pure and unguarded. A moment full of joy, and without thinking, I turned to share it—only to find the space beside me empty.

The day it came from had been good, my children happy, the world generous. This day was smaller, edged with problems and the unfamiliar weight of my situation. The circumstances had nothing in common, yet the absence felt similar. It settled in beside me, gentle but unmistakable, as it always had.

With each step by the lake, I steadied myself, making peace with standing on my own two feet.

God willing, that may change one day. But not today. Today required something else. I had to refocus on the life directly in front of me.

I didn't want to call my son or my friends. I'd been gone less than twenty-four hours, and I knew exactly what the response would be. No, this road had been chosen for many reasons. I would not let a lousy battery stop me. It was that simple.

That evening, I met the couple camped beside me. When I stepped out to turn off the truck, they waved me over. I decided that one good evening on my first stop would count as a win. I poured a glass of wine, grabbed my chair, and joined them by their fire.

Her name was Renee. His was Dale. Renee traveled in a Class C; Dale drove an impressive Jeep outfitted for serious off-road adventures, winch and all. They admitted they'd been watching me—kindly— and gently called out my newbie status. Given the open layout of the campground, I suspected not much went unnoticed.

We sat by the fire exchanging stories into the night. They offered practical advice, the kind that only seems obvious after something goes wrong. Dale told me to carry a portable battery charger in case I ever lost phone service. "Learned that one the hard way," he said, laughing. "Dead phone, dead truck battery, middle of nowhere Nevada. Took half a day before someone came along." I made a quiet mental note.

Renee told me she'd ridden her motorcycle across the country and through Canada multiple times. I listened, captivated. Though at least a generation younger than me, she seemed to have always known what she wanted, and what she didn't. I couldn't help wondering what difference a single generation could make in the liberation of the mind and soul.

They talked about people they'd met on the road and the friendships that had formed. Renee told me to pay attention when offers are made, like Dale's casual mention I could park on his fifty acres anytime I passed through.

"People don't offer that," she said, "unless they see you as good people."

They also talked about trusting your instincts. Dale said it matter-of-factly, like someone who had already tested the idea. "Anytime something feels off, I move," he said. "Doesn't matter if I can explain it or not."

It was a skill I understood I had neglected. I had been taught to obey, not to listen to myself. Sitting there by the fire, it occurred to me that I had set something more powerful in motion than any itinerary.

They used the word *mindfulness*, a word I knew, but one I revisited more deeply later. Awareness. Presence without judgment. I thought about the battery problem. I'd gathered information, stayed calm, and made decisions without spiraling, not because I felt confident, but because I kept moving forward anyway.

I contemplated the difference between Renee and Dale and the people who had filled my life. Of course they were different. I was in a new environment, doing something unfamiliar to everyone I'd known. I saw them as adventurers—capable, grounded, unafraid. What struck me wasn't that they seemed extraordinary, but that they appeared comfortable inside uncertainty. And for the first time, I could imagine becoming one.

The question lingered: how much of an adventurer did I want to become?

I went to bed on the second night of my new beginning with most of my self-recrimination put to rest. I'd made mistakes, but I'd also been encouraged. I'd been reminded that systems deserve scrutiny, that learning takes time—and that getting this far on my own counted for something.

The next morning, coffee in hand, I felt good. Even with the battery failure and my obvious inexperience, I decided that not knowing everything yet was acceptable.

That belief was tested an hour later when I tried to start the truck, and nothing happened. In my frustration the night before, I had forgotten to unplug the trailer.

This, I learned, was the unglamorous side of choosing a life without instructions.

Renee and Dale helped jump-start the truck and reminded me,

again, about the portable charger. With many thanks, I was on my way, hopeful I would meet many more acquaintances along the road.

Theory had set me in motion. Reality had its own way of teaching the rest.

CHAPTER 8 — LISTENING TO THE UNEASE

What unsettles you is often where truth is asking to be heard

Reality rarely matches the dream. I had pictured this day so many times: leaving California with little responsibility and nothing ahead of me but what I chose. Instead, it was a rockier start, like learning to drive a stick shift and popping the clutch again and again. You lurch forward, stall out, and have to start over. It became second nature, but getting there was its own story. The stretch between California and Vancouver Island felt exactly like that.

This was the day I left California. I felt raw, exposed, and very much on my own. It was perfect.

I was looking forward to hitting the highway, hopeful for the ease that always seemed to return once I was moving. I successfully navigated out of the campground, but immediately took a wrong turn, turning a simple errand into the long way around just to reach the gas station. I couldn't help but laugh at myself. I had left plenty of time. I had a reservation for two nights just over the border in Ashland, and my only goal was to unhitch before nightfall.

Once I corrected my route, the road narrowed into a scenic back way. My father used to do that too—take what he called a *shortcut* that always turned out to be the scenic route. Maybe I came by my fondness for back roads honestly. As it turned out, the less-traveled roads would become a theme.

Pulling into a gas station with the trailer for the first time, flashes of fiery catastrophe flickered through my thoughts. I parked along the street and watched other rigs come and go—where they entered, how wide they swung their turns, which aisles and pumps they chose. I took a deep breath and followed their examples. While the gas pumped, I stood still and studied the surrounding space. That was the key: assessing the space correctly. I could do that. Another fear dismantled. And that was that.

The moment I merged onto the interstate, I felt the familiar lift. Driving restored—and reshaped—the lightness I'd felt when I first left. Music up, *Traveler* leading the way. Nothing else mattered. Problems receded. While I was moving, I was free of everything but being. That entire day remains vivid to me—the serenity, the peace, the happiness. Crossing into Oregon felt like stepping into a new, wider world.

The campground I'd booked barely resembled its photos. Maintenance looked neglected. Grass stood tall. Paint peeled. Fence boards were missing. Gardens leaned more toward compost than decoration. A few painted buses sat awkwardly in the middle of the grounds.

My gut told me to leave. I stayed.

The office clerk was disgruntled, another warning, louder this time. I ignored it. I unhitched and settled in, a process that took over an hour.

Just after dusk, there was a knock on my door.

That alone made me hesitate. One of the safety rules I'd read warned against knocking on closed doors at night. Through the small window, I saw a boy, maybe ten years old, trying to peer inside. I opened the door only a few inches. When I asked if I could help him, he asked how many televisions and computers I had.

A chill slipped down my spine. I knew an adult had sent him. He was probably meant to look, not ask. I said something brief—no thank you—then closed the door. I leaned my head against the frame and whispered a small prayer for the child.

Sleep came in fragments that night. I reminded myself again and again that it was the trailer they were interested in, not me. Still, every sound felt amplified. At first light, I hitched up and left.

An hour north, I pulled into a KOA and stayed for the day and night. I needed to reassess.

I was just talking about trusting my instincts, my most important safety tool. And here I was, ignoring them right out of the gate. Not once, but twice. Each warning should have stopped me. I hadn't even paused to acknowledge how I felt, let alone validate it.

That had to change. What I sensed mattered.

This wasn't something I needed to learn; it was a way of life I had to adopt. I promised myself I would carry that awareness forward, steadier and wiser.

The next day, I found an RV repair shop and had the batteries replaced. Then I moved on.

Things break and you learn to fix them. You keep going. Choosing an unsanctioned life meant becoming my own safety net.

As the miles passed, the road smoothed out and my days found a rhythm.

Through Harvest Hosts, I camped behind a bar next to a volunteer fire department in a small Oregon town where karaoke echoed through the rain. I spent two nights on a farm in Washington—mornings with sheep, goats, geese, chickens, and llamas; evenings around a fire listening to strangers' stories.

One couple from Austria had shipped their rig to South America and zigzagged north for four years. They were headed to Alaska. There was a quiet steadiness about them—an ease I didn't yet recognize in myself— that drew me in. When I expressed awe at what they'd accomplished— and questioned my own abilities—the husband smiled and offered one word: *yet.* I took it with me.

Maneuvering the trailer remained my greatest challenge. At a campground near the base of Mount Baker, it took an exasperating hour to back into my site. But I did it. After that, I became more selective about the sites I chose.

Before I knew it, Vancouver Island, where my sister Sandy lives, lay ahead. I looked forward to the satisfaction of pulling in after towing all the way from California—including towing the trailer onto a ferry. The nerves came and went. When I finally arrived and jumped out of the truck to hug my sister, the words slipped out before I could stop them: "I did it."

The next part of my trip was still undefined, but I could feel the theory behind my journey beginning to give way to experience.

CHAPTER 9 — THE ROAD WIDENS

Once I found my footing in the months that followed, stopping felt unnatural, as if decades of held tension had suddenly been set free. Once earned, momentum resisted stillness. It was like the snap of a slingshot: swift, decisive. I couldn't stay anywhere long enough to settle before the road tugged again, plans shifting easily—sometimes mid-route—as I chose momentum over certainty. That first year unfolded exactly this way: movement first, understanding later.

What caught me off guard wasn't the logistics—the miles, the schedules, the constant recalculation—but the internal shift. It was learning to trust what I felt without submitting every impulse to an internal committee for approval. Me, myself, and I conducted exhausting negotiations over whether a desire was even acceptable. I resented how easily I could think, "I like this," and immediately feel obligated to justify the wanting.

Then came moments that bypassed the debate entirely. I hopped aboard a haunted trolley tour in Savannah, Georgia—alone, late at night—something my former rulebook would have flagged as unsafe or improper. I did it anyway, with little hesitation. Each time I made a choice like that, the voice of doubt receded, replaced not by certainty but by a growing trust that what felt right did not require defense.

As the months passed, I met people who seemed to live this way instinctively—adventurers who trusted themselves without apology.

Some traveled light, some with companions, some alone. They didn't always know what lay ahead, but they understood how to respond when it arrived. I admired that orientation. I paid attention. Slowly, without announcing itself, that way of moving through the world began to feel natural.

In Darby, Montana, a small town tucked beneath the Bitterroot Range where the air smelled of sun-warmed pine needles, dusty soil, and the dry sweetness of valley grass, I decided to join some of the other campers under a large gazebo around a community fire. A man had set up in the back of his pickup, playing guitar and singing. As I chatted, I met some who were working in the area, others taking a break from hiking the Continental Divide, and campers from all over, like me. Simple, but one of those warm evenings you don't forget—even though everyone was a stranger when you sat down.

This is where I met Robbi and Mark. They were from Australia and had challenged themselves to explore the States in a year, traveling and living out of an SUV. Compared to them, my twenty-five-foot trailer felt extravagant. We had little in common on paper—age, setup, pace— yet our motivations aligned. Much of what they experienced wasn't planned; it revealed itself along the way. We were both trying to live inside what felt honest. That encounter stayed with me. It reminded me that freedom doesn't scale; it simply fits.

Not all companionship on the road came from strangers. That summer, my granddaughter, Layeli, joined me for part of the journey, and something in the adventure widened for both of us. I wanted to share with her not only the places I was discovering, but what lies just beyond what feels familiar when met with a little courage. Pushing limits, after all, was part of this journey.

I picked her up at the airport in Seattle and we traveled together across Washington, Idaho, and down through Montana. We parasailed over Lake Coeur d'Alene, rode horses in the Bitterroot Range of the

Rockies, white-water rafted the Clark Fork River outside Missoula, and went ziplining. We explored craft fairs, steakhouses, trailheads, and hot springs. Each time she did something she hadn't imagined for herself, I watched her confidence blossom. When my granddaughter boarded the plane home in Bozeman, I hoped she carried a new light within her. I certainly did.

Months earlier she had asked whether I was running away. Out on the road together, I hoped she was beginning to see what I had been running toward.

Being alone on the road didn't always feel empowering. Loneliness surfaced at times, especially when something went wrong and there was no one else to consult. Yet solitude also demanded clarity. When I was alone, there was no consensus to reach. I assessed the situation, acted, adapted, and moved forward. Over time, that process built a quiet confidence—one rooted less in bravery than in accumulated competence.

Not every interaction reinforced that confidence. Occasionally, I encountered suspicion or projection—assumptions about why a woman would be traveling alone or what she must be seeking. Years earlier, I might have softened myself to make others more comfortable, explaining or justifying choices that required no defense. Now, I simply walked on. Their interpretations belonged to them, not to me.

The road kept widening my sense of companionship in unexpected ways. A few times I joined rallies sponsored by different Airstream groups. It was another opportunity to learn more about my trailer and to meet new people. One morning I was having coffee outside the trailer when a couple passed slowly with two dogs. The dogs ambled over to say hello, and I met them halfway, kneeling to pet them. I had noticed the couple's unhurried walks before, but that morning I learned they had taken both dogs in to care for them in the last months of their lives—a kind of hospice. The tenderness of it caught me off guard. Watching them walk away, I felt tears rise. Even now, telling it, I do.

Some moments arrived gently. Others announced themselves without warning.

One afternoon, after settling into a campground, I found myself doubled over with abdominal pain. Standing alone in my trailer, I did what the road had already taught me to do: I assessed. I checked distances, identified the nearest hospital, stocked the fridge, obtained medicine, and rested. Each day, I walked a little farther. When it became clear I needed more time, I extended my stay. It felt practical, not dramatic. And that, I knew, was the point.

Afterward, I assembled a small over-the-counter pharmacy and kept it close. Alone, preparation becomes less about fear and more about kindness to your future self.

As my strength returned, I wandered with greater intention. I stopped more often. I lingered when something caught my attention. Once, I pulled into a historic site simply because it was on my left and I could. It wasn't the last time I diverted on a whim. I pulled over for whatever interested me—historic sites, roadside oddities, small towns, nothing at all—because I wanted to. Freedom, I came to understand, wasn't found only in motion. It also lived in choosing when not to rush past something meaningful.

The moment that stayed with me longest came during a jeep tour across open prairie where the grass rolled in long amber waves toward distant hills, when our vehicle was forced to stop completely. A herd of buffalo moved around us, close enough that there was nothing to do but wait.

They were massive, awkward, entirely themselves. What fascinated me most wasn't their size, but their order. Older females led the herd—steady, experienced, making decisions collectively. The bulls appeared briefly during mating season, disrupted everything, and then wandered off. Order returned.

I smiled.

Long stretches of calm leadership shaped by age and experience. Brief eruptions of chaos. Then balance. No apologies.

I thought about how little respect our culture affords its elders, how easily experience is dismissed in favor of urgency or volume. I wondered how many systems I had lived inside that confused authority with wisdom, mistaking unearned certainty for leadership.

When the herd moved on, so did we. But the imprint remained.

By then, it felt as though I was no longer collecting experiences. They were collecting me—reshaping how I responded, how I decided, how I trusted myself, and where I chose to stand. Theory had done what it could. The rest, I was learning through experience.

CHAPTER 10 — STAYING SAFE ON THE ROAD

Protection lives between faith, intuition, and action

I didn't set out to become an expert in safety. I set out to become free. But freedom on the road turned out to be more than courage and scenery—it was habits, checks, and logical decisions that kept me moving. I learned to trust the space between faith and preparation. One without the other becomes either fear or recklessness. Out there, safety became its own kind of balance—earned mile by mile, mistake by mistake.

Some Things I Learned the Hard Way

Never remove the clip out of the hitch post. Ever. *(Sheridan, Wyoming)*

The chocks go in first when you park and come out last before you pull away. *(Custer, South Dakota)*

Stabilizer jacks are the last thing down after unhitching and the first thing up when hitching. *(Galveston, Texas)*

Always double-check that windows are locked and cabinet doors are secured. *(Highway 80, Wyoming; Highway 40, Kentucky; Highway 84, Texas)*

Are You Sure It's Safe?

Before the journey began, people asked the same question: *Are you sure it's safe to do this alone?*

What I learned is that safety was never a single thing to be measured. It was a practice. A mindset. A rhythm learned slowly—through mistakes, small panics, and the humbling experience of changing direction at sixty-five. Safety wasn't fear. It was expanded awareness; confidence built one mile at a time.

While I may have been traveling alone, I wasn't traveling unnoticed. My family and a good friend tracked me. They checked in. They shared the journey from afar.

My sister played a larger role than I often admit. On travel days, she followed my progress until I finally stopped for the night. On quieter backcountry roads—often the ones I preferred—she sometimes stayed on the phone with me, watching my route by satellite view, narrating the landscape as it unfolded and calling out the distance to the next fuel stop. More than once, her voice came with a warning when she sensed I was heading into something I hadn't fully anticipated.

One time, I took a road through the Rockies without enough research. It tightened into a twisting stretch with only a few big rigs, no turnoffs, and almost no shoulder. Near the peak, snow started falling, and visibility dropped. There was nowhere to stop and no way to turn back. I had no choice but to keep going. My hands were locked on the steering wheel while Sandy stayed on the line, steady and calm, helping me breathe and focus until I was through.

I was by myself in that cab—but not alone on that road.

It grounded me more than once. And a few times, it mattered in ways I didn't fully grasp until later.

Machines Don't Care About Your Feelings

I learned quickly that safety begins not with pepper spray or late-night vigilance, but with the machinery that carries your life. A truck and trailer do not care if you're tired, nervous, or unsure. They want what they want—and if you ignore them, they let you know.

When I first encountered terms like *tow capacity* and *payload*, I assumed they simply meant the truck could pull the trailer. I didn't yet understand that they meant pulling it safely up hills, down steep grades, through crosswinds, with a full water tank and every pound of "just in case" cargo onboard. It felt like a physics class I had barely survived decades earlier.

The same was true of tongue weight, axle balance, hitching, and that insistent little device called a brake controller. None of these existed in my vocabulary before, and suddenly they held the power to determine whether my trailer and I stayed upright on the highway.

But complicated systems have a gift: once you learn them, they return confidence you didn't know you were missing. I found that operating them was far more instructive than reading about them.

For months, I didn't even know where the brake controller was— hidden in plain sight, unlabeled, silently waiting for me to learn its language. Once I did, fear loosened its grip.

For nearly a year, I didn't understand how the heat pump worked.

The first time I latched the hitch myself—correctly attaching the stabilizer bars, checking the chains, locking the coupler, testing the lights, and feeling the trailer settle behind me—it felt as if the universe whispered, *See? You can do this.*

Campgrounds, Corners, and Paying Attention

Safety on the road is partly about people, but just as much about place.

I learned to choose campsites with instinct and an eye on the exit— nose out, door locked, light used intentionally. On when needed, off when quiet was welcome.

The more peaceful campgrounds aren't always the polished ones. Often, they're the more organic parks: gravel roads, aging bathhouses, fewer frills. Those places tend to attract people who respect silence, mornings, and shared land.

Traveling alone required a broader awareness that extended beyond the campground.

It isn't wise to hike solo, especially in bear country.

It isn't wise to wander unfamiliar cities without considering where you park, or where your feet carry you after dark.

And if you don't see the usual small animals—squirrels, birds, rabbits—it often means larger ones are nearby.

In unfamiliar places, I learned to pause. To observe. To let the surroundings introduce themselves before stepping in.

If a site felt off, I moved. No explanations. No guilt. No apologies to the inner voice that once whispered I was being dramatic.

My intuition does not require permission.

Weather, Wind, and What I Can't Control

You don't realize how big the sky is until you're driving beneath it with a twenty-five-foot silver tube trailing behind you—and your weather app beeps with a *take-shelter* warning. Out there, the sky isn't a backdrop; it's a presence. Weather patterns became something to notice, especially for someone from California, where they rarely insist on being taken seriously.

Weather apps and their warnings slipped into my morning ritual, though I learned quickly how thin that reassurance could be.

In Nebraska, somewhere near the largest ball of twine, I was camping beside a wide, wind-swept lake when, like a light switch, everything went dark. I'm pretty sure I screamed. Lightning tore through the sky while thunder—so fierce it rocked the trailer—seemed to pin it in place. It was nonstop, with no sense of when it might move on. I had no idea what to expect, and for the first time, I wondered whether I would make it through the night. My dear friend Jeanette stayed on the phone with me for the next two hours. There was no warning that time.

Outside Fort Smith, Arkansas, I slept behind a Cracker Barrel. A little after dawn, my phone began beeping with a hurricane warning that quickly escalated to *take shelter*. I gathered a few essentials, locked the rig, and spent an hour in the restaurant bathroom. When it passed, the sky cleared. I ate breakfast among the others as if nothing unusual had happened.

Wind became a teacher. It doesn't announce itself; it corrects you. A sudden gust on an open highway can humble you in seconds. The first time my trailer swayed, my stomach dropped. Passing trucks could do it too, an invisible shove reminding me who held the advantage.

Rain demanded patience. In southeastern Texas, storms lingered—heavy rain drumming against the truck roof, thunder rolling across the humid air, lightning flashing so brightly it turned everything white. Warnings bloomed across my phone. I found a campground and stayed. During a brief clearing, I unhitched and hooked up the utilities. The storm stayed a week. The place turned beautiful. I stayed another.

A tornado warning still feels unreal when you're from California, until it isn't. At Lake Eufaula in Oklahoma, the alert arrived just as my cousin banged on my door to help me hitch and leave. Hours later, the tornado passed directly over the place where I'd been camping.

By the time I was driving through the Cascades in Washington, the lesson was settling in. Wet cedar and moss hung in the air as rain blurred the road ahead. A cloudy day tightened into rain and wind, visibility collapsing on a crowded Highway 90. There was nothing to fix. You slow down. You hold steady.

Over time, patterns emerged: stay wide when a rig passes, don't fight the sway, reduce speed, avoid crosswinds—and when the choice exists, get off the road and wait. Waiting, I realized, wasn't quitting. It was listening.

Over time, I understood that safety isn't the absence of danger.

It's the presence of wider awareness.

People: the Good, the Odd, and the Ones You Avoid

Traveling alone taught me to read people quickly—how they moved, how they looked at me, how close they stood.

For added security, my children, my friend Jeanette, and my sister had access to my location. If something happened, someone could at least say where I'd last been.

I never announced that I was alone.

I never shared my route ahead of time.

If someone asked too many questions, my answers became short, vague, and deliberately unhelpful.

Most people were kind. Many admired the rig. Some were simply curious. A few tested boundaries.

Once, after pumping gas, a man appeared at my door window and questioned why I was alone, mentioning my California plates. I chose calm over confrontation: I answered just enough to disengage, put the truck in drive, and left.

Another time, after a wrong turn on the west side of the Blue Ridge Parkway, I pulled over to deal with a stubborn map app. A man stopped and, from a respectable distance, asked if I needed help and quickly solved the problem. Kindness prevailed more often than not.

The road turned out to differ greatly from the stories people tell. Campgrounds were filled with families, retirees, hikers, mechanics, dog lovers—and women who had finally stopped waiting for permission.

Still, I kept my doors locked, my keys close, and my truck positioned for a clean departure—not out of fear, but out of respect for myself and the freedom I had claimed.

Health, Illness, and Listening

COVID taught me early that safety begins with the body—what it can do, what it can't, and when it needs me to stop.

On the road, I learned to rest without guilt. To hydrate. To carry what I might need. To stop believing toughness was the goal.

Sometimes safety looked like lying down and waiting.

Sometimes it meant medical intervention.

I tripped while clearing the area around my hookups and broke my arm seriously enough to require surgery—plates, screws, and the firm instruction not to drive. Not that you can wrangle a hitch with one arm.

What made it harder was where I was: on Vancouver Island, out of the country, suddenly injured and unable to move on. The medical care was excellent, but it came with an immediate financial reckoning. Bills arrived before certainty. Trust became part of the treatment.

This was intuition too, just not the kind that urges motion. It asked for stillness. For listening. For allowing safety to look different from what it had on the road. Phone calls and paperwork replaced miles. Forward motion paused, but my awareness did not.

Even so, I was held. The campground extended my stay. A grocery store was within walking distance. My sister and niece were close. I healed on the beach in cooler air, time stretching in ways I hadn't planned, while friends back home endured the weight of summer heat.

Whether or not I wanted to, I stopped. I rested. I healed.

Preparedness felt like another form of listening, one that mattered long before anything went wrong.

Faith Beneath Everything

No matter how careful I became, there was always another layer of safety—one I couldn't engineer.

Call it faith.

Call it intuition.

Call it the peaceful companionship of something larger.

There were mornings I stepped outside and felt held. Nights I locked the door and knew I wasn't alone. Moments on the road when I whispered, *stay with me*, and felt an answer.

Safety, I came to understand, is a partnership between preparation and grace. Over time, it became less a checklist and more a way of being—alert but unafraid, watchful but not closed.

Slowly, mile by mile, I became the woman who no longer asked, *Is it safe?*

Instead, I learned to say: *I am.*

CHAPTER 11 — EXPERIENCE IS A PATIENT TEACHER

Wisdom rarely arrives ahead of us

Experience has a way of quietly teaching what anticipation cannot. Looking back now, there are a few things I understand more clearly—things that wouldn't have stopped me but might have spared me a little worry. Still, I'm not sure I would have believed them then. Some things only make sense once the road feels familiar.

I can see how much of this journey was built on faith, silent instinct, and stubborn hope. I had plans, of course—timelines, lists, budgets, tasks lined up like dominoes—but plans are tidy, and real life rarely is. Had I known then what I know now, I might have moved through those early months with more grace, more patience for myself, and fewer frantic internet searches about electrical systems and propane tanks.

In hindsight, nothing arrived too early or too late. The understanding came afterward, not before—like lanterns lighting the path behind me rather than the one ahead.

Still, if I could gather these insights in one place, I would tell my earlier self that downsizing isn't a weekend project—it's a full emotional unraveling. Letting go of possessions was easy compared to the stories attached to them. Each drawer became an inventory, each object demanding a decision: keep, carry, or release. What made it harder was the subtle fear that without the object, the memory might fade. I thought downsizing meant clearing out clutter. In reality, it meant sifting through decades of identity—and deciding which parts of it held the value to carry forward.

Another realization came quickly: preparing my body mattered just as much as my finances. I had walked regularly and stayed active, but none of that prepared me for the particular physical demands of life on the road. Hitching and unhitching required strength I hadn't trained for. Climbing in and out of the truck bed, lifting gear, stabilizing the trailer—each task seemed minor on its own, yet together they created a constant strain. I didn't recognize how many muscles were involved until they protested, spasming or aching in ways that made one thing clear: endurance isn't built by intention alone, but by conditioning for the work you actually perform.

I wish I had known how much the map you travel by shapes the journey. It isn't simply a matter of directions, but of terrain. Coming from California, I was accustomed to relatively straightforward routes. Crossing the country required something more nuanced: not just a destination, but an understanding of the road there. I started asking different questions. Was the grade manageable or a white-knuckle route? Were there safe pullouts and passing lanes? Was refueling an issue?

I learned how powerful bartering could be before I left on my journey. Trading used appliances for moving help, an entertainment center for carpet cleaning—those minor exchanges created more relief than I expected. On the road, that instinct took on a new shape. I began picking up and carrying small offerings: hand-carved kitchen spoons, sets of hand-painted notes with matching envelopes—objects made slowly and with attention. They took up little space, but they carried intention. Every so often, when I needed help in a campground—a repair, an extra set of hands—those small gifts became my way of reciprocating. Not as payment, but as acknowledgment. An exchange for kindness lent.

Illness shaped my beginning more than I expected. COVID forced me into stillness, into surrender, into a gentler start than the one I had planned. I thought I would arrive strong and prepared; instead, I arrived humbled. Being sick on the road clarified what preparation really meant—keeping medicine close, knowing where help was, and allowing my body the time it needed to recover. What felt like a delay became an education in care, both practical and necessary.

What I didn't expect was how often fear and freedom would arrive together. That first morning in the trailer, curtains drawn wide, coffee in hand, I felt both the terror of the unknown and the pure adrenaline of stepping into a life I had feared to dream. I wish I could have told myself then that trembling and triumph are not opposites, but companions.

I wish I had known that children and grandchildren ask the questions we avoid asking ourselves. My granddaughter's small voice—"Gma, are you running away?"—cut through every justification I had assembled. In answering her, I told the truth to myself.

Courage, I learned, rarely arrives as a single leap, but as a series of small decisions. Hitch the trailer. Unhitch the trailer. Rest when sick. Move forward anyway. Trust faith. Trust myself. Each step carried its own quiet bravery.

These are the things I wish I had known. But had I known them too soon—or all at once—I might have disrupted the balance of the adventure itself. Sometimes the only way to build a new life is to walk into it with openness rather than certainty—heart first, faith forward— and allow understanding to follow.

And that is exactly what I did.

EPILOGUE

Freedom reveals itself in the miles we dare to chance

Women of my generation were raised in a world where only a small fraction of us went to college, and even fewer finished. Most married young, had children early, and learned to step in and out of the workforce as life dictated. We were expected to shape our futures around others—husbands, children, parents, obligations—long before anyone asked what we wanted for ourselves.

So when I chose a different path decades later—one shaped by independence, self-trust, and the wide-open road—it wasn't simply a personal change. It was a rewriting of the script my generation had been handed.

At first, I believed travel would offer little more than new scenery. What it gave me instead was space—to think, to listen, to notice who I was without the constant hum of expectation. The miles softened the edges of fear. The landscapes rearranged my understanding of possibility. Solitude taught me the difference between being alone and being free.

I learned that the country is far bigger, kinder, and more beautiful than the stories we are told. Strangers became helpers. Helpers became friends. The road became a teacher, if I allowed it to be. I discovered I could tow my own home, navigate weather, recover from mistakes, and laugh at myself more often than I ever had before.

Travel became a kind of prayer.

The mountains answered questions I hadn't yet learned to hold.

The sky—wide and unapologetic—reminded me that a woman is allowed to take up space.

I sat beneath stars so bright they felt like a promise.

What surprised me most was not what I learned about the road, but what I learned about myself. I learned to listen—to my instincts, my limits, my longings—without immediately negotiating them away. That kind of knowing doesn't belong to youth. It belongs to the brave.

Every mile became a quiet conversation between who I had been and who I trusted myself to be. Some days I felt like a student. Other days, a survivor. Many days, simply a woman grateful to watch light spill across mountains she had never seen before, or to drive a highway suspended between sky and land. I no longer felt like an outlaw for wanting something unorthodox. I had stepped into my own authority— into my full maturity.

Somewhere between deserts and coastlines, forests and winding mountain passes, I came to a certainty I now carry with me:

It had never been too late to choose my own life.

Not at sixty-five.

Not at seventy.

Not ever.

The balance I was searching for—the space between the weight of living fully human and the light that stands quietly behind us—was never waiting beyond the next horizon. It was built in the doing: in hitching and unhitching, in wrong turns and weather warnings, in learning systems I once found intimidating, in believing my instincts when they spoke, and in the kindness shared along the way.

Confidence replaced hesitation. I stopped asking for permission. I began trusting the life directly in front of me. And I found faith in my pen.

Freedom was not the destination; it was the doorway.

And stepping through it changed everything.

ACKNOWLEDGMENTS

This journey may have been mine to experience, but I did not travel it alone.

To my family, who kept track of me and checked in regularly—my son, who was half in awe and half in concern; my daughter and granddaughters, who spent weekends camping with me; my brother Bill and his wife Debbie, who welcomed me and my stories each time I passed their way; my niece Kate, who introduced me to my first music festival; and my sister Sandy, who faithfully followed along from afar. Without their support, this journey would have been far more difficult.

To my dear friend Jeanette, who showed up quietly during those first difficult days in Napa with food, medicine, and encouragement, and who continued to check in as I made my way down the road. Her support was steady, generous, and far beyond what I could have expected.

Special thanks to Bev, who stepped in at a difficult moment to help get me on the road, and to my friends Stephanie and Kathy for their encouragement—both for the journey and for this project.

Finding quality assistance for the maintenance and repair of the Airstream was a bumpy road and came with some difficult days. Eventually, I found people I could trust—those who were fair and who believed in doing the right thing. I want to especially thank Vinnie and his crew at Vinnie's in Sacramento, California, and Albert, his sister Kenia, and their crew at MEL Trailers in Placentia, California.

Finally, thank you to Ema Barnes and Caryn Rivadeneira for their thoughtful editorial guidance, and to Nuno Moreira at NM Design for bringing this project to life through its cover and interior design.

ABOUT THE AUTHOR

Deb Hazlett writes about resilience, self-reliance, and the quiet turning points that reshape a life. *Before Tomorrow* grew from her decision to step away from the expected and follow a different path—one measured in miles, uncertainty, and discovery. She is currently at work on her novel *Where the Roots Hold*.